MIDGET SUBMARINES

Paul J. Kemp

Front cover illustration: *XT1* comes alongside her depot ship in Holy Loch in February 1944. The XT-Craft were built for training purposes only. They were not fitted with cargo release gear or a night periscope and the induction mast was a fixed structure which could not be lowered. Eighteen units were ordered but only six were completed, the remainder being cancelled at the end of the war. The senior officer standing on the casing is Rear-Admiral Claude Barry, the head of the Royal Navy's Submarine Service. (IWM A.21692)

Back cover illustrations: Top: An X-Craft, possibly *X24*, under way in 1944 during a demonstration trip for the benefit of the Press. Fourteen similar X-Craft were built: the prototypes *X3* and *X4* followed by *X5* to *X10*, which were all lost in Operation 'Source' and lastly *X20* to *X25*. They all served in Home Waters and their successes can be conveniently summed up as one 42,000-ton battleship crippled, one merchant ship and a floating dock sunk and an invasion fleet safely conducted to its destination. (IWM A.22903)

Below: 285 *Seehunden* were built: eighteen of them are shown here at Kiel after the German surrender. It has been estimated that 35 were lost in action or as a result of bad weather. Claims that *Seehunden* sank or damaged some 100,000 tons of Allied shipping between January and May 1945 are difficult to reconcile with the records. (IWM A.28973)

MIDGET SUBMARINES

Paul J. Kemp

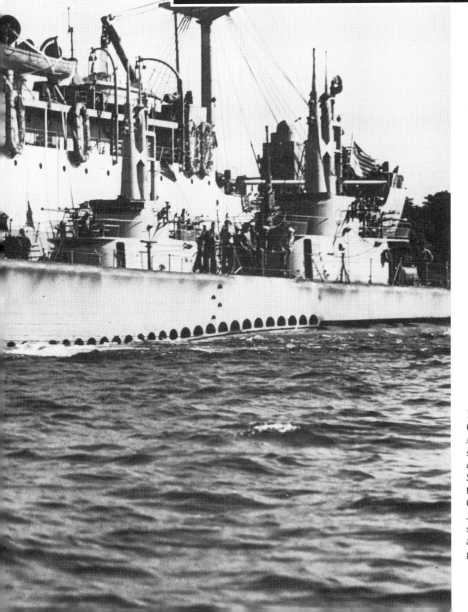

ARMS AND
ARMOUR

1. David and Goliath: a tiny XE-Craft is dwarfed by three large American *Gato*-class submarines lying along the depot ship HMS *Bonaventure* at Sydney in 1945. Nevertheless, the men who operated the XE-Craft were described by Admiral James Fife, senior US submarine officer in the Pacific, as 'the little guys with a lotta guts!' (IWM ABS.896)

2. Appearances are deceptive. Admiral Sir Andrew Cunningham takes the salute at the morning ceremony of 'Colours' aboard his flagship HMS *Queen Elizabeth* at Alexandria on the morning of 19 December 1941. Cunningham had ordered the traditional ceremony to go ahead with guard and band as a bluff in the hope that no-one would notice that on the previous night Italian 'Human Torpedoes' had crippled his flagship and HMS *Valiant* and thereby altered the balance of naval power in the Mediterranean overnight. In his memoirs Cunningham noted that 'One cannot but admire the cold-blooded bravery of these Italians.' (IWM A.7052)

3. During the First World War many naval powers had submarines which were 'midget' even by the standards of the day. The photograph shows the Italian midget submarine *Alpha* at the Arsenal at Venice in 1913. *Alpha* was never formally commissioned into the *Regia Marina*, being used only for trials. She was followed by the larger A and B classes, designed solely for harbour defence among the islands of the Venetian lagoon, which saw service during the Great War. The potential of this sort of craft for taking the war into the enemy's harbour was not yet realized. (Museo Storico Navale, Venice)

▲2   ▼3

INTRODUCTION

Arms and Armour Press
A Cassell Imprint
Villiers House, 41–47 Strand,
London WC2N 5JE.

Distributed in the USA by Sterling
Publishing Co. Inc., 387 Park
Avenue South, New York, NY
10016-8810.

Distributed in Australia by
Capricorn Link (Australia) Pty. Ltd,
P.O. Box 665, Lane Cove, New
South Wales 2066.

British Library Cataloguing in
Publication Data
Midget submarines. – (Fotofax).
1. Naval operations by
submarines
. Kemp, Paul II. Series
SBN 1-85409-092-5

Line illustrations by Marija Batica.

Designed and edited by DAG
Publications Ltd. Designed by
David Gibbons; edited by Michael
Boxall; layout by Anthony A.
Evans; typeset by Typesetters
(Birmingham) Ltd and Ronset
Typesetters Ltd; camerawork by
M&E; Reproductions, North
Cambridge, Essex; printed and
bound in Great Britain by The
Alden Press, Oxford.

Midget submarines – the term is used in its widest sense and includes human torpedoes, semi-submersibles and midget submarines proper – are a subject of compelling interest. On the morning of 1 November 1918 two Italian officers swimming alongside a torpedo-like craft called *Mignatta*, penetrated the Austrian harbour at Pola and attached a mine to the hull of the Austrian flagship *Viribus Unitis*. At 0620 the charge detonated with a 'dull roar' and the mighty battleship with her armament of twelve 12in guns rolled over and sank. This was the first successful attack by a midget submarine and although the sinking of *Viribus Unitis* came too late to have any effect on the war, Austria having already requested an armistice, the daring raid was to be the inspiration for further development in this field.

The origins of the midget submarine go back a good deal further than 1918, however. The true 'father' of the midget was an American, David Bushnell, who constructed an egg-shaped craft called *Turtle* which was armed with a clockwork-fuzed 150lb charge of gunpowder which would be attached to the wooden hull of the target by means of an auger operated from within *Turtle*. In September 1776 *Turtle*, operated by Sergeant Ezra Lee, made a number of attacks on British ships anchored off New York. Legends abound of how Lee's efforts were frustrated by the copper sheathing of the British ships but reliable information is harder to find.

In the early days of submarine development, the primitive technology meant that all submarines were 'midgets' and designed with the primary role of attacking or defending anchorages. Russia and Italy were the two powers who developed small submarines for this purpose. There was also a British design named *Devastator* – a cross between a torpedo and a submarine – which was never constructed. It was only with the construction of large ocean-going patrol submarines that a separate stream of development of 'midget' submarines was able to proceed. Although various midget submarines, the Italian A and B classes and the Russian 'Holland' type, were operational during the First World War, their offensive potential was not realized: the success of *Mignatta* was but an isolated incident. It was only during the Second World War that midgets were employed to any effect.

During the 1939–45 conflict all the major belligerent navies with the exception of those of the United States, France and the Soviet Union employed midget submarines. The absence of the Soviet Union from this field may seem surprising in view of Russia's pioneering work in this area, but the highly individualistic nature of midget submarine operations did not suit the centralized Soviet command structure.

Three distinct kinds of midget submarine made their appearance during the Second World War: human torpedoes (the Italian *Maiale* and British Chariot); small submersibles (the German *Biber* and associated craft, British Welman and Japanese *Kaiten*) and true midget submarines (British X Craft, Italian CA/CB, Japanese *Ko-Hyoteki* and German *Seehund*).

It was the Italians who led the way with the development of the *Maiale*, two-man human torpedoes which were used to such deadly effect at Alexandria and

Gibraltar. However the activities of the Italian CA and CB midget submarines deserve attention and in particular the plan to carry CA.2 on the deck of the submarine *Leonardo Da Vinci* and use her to attack shipping in New York harbour. Trials proved the scheme to be workable but the plan was never put into action.

The Royal Navy had shown no interest in midget submarines in peacetime. It was only when the Prime Minister, Winston Churchill, demanded that steps be taken to deal with the German battleship *Tirpitz* that the Admiralty began to investigate these weapons seriously. Britain emulated the Italians in the construction of human torpedoes, called 'Chariots' in British service, and midget submarines, the Welman and the X-Craft. The Welman was a useless craft which ought never to have been built, but the four-man X-Craft was a potent weapon of war. British midgets saw action in all three theatres of war and scored significant successes, in particular the crippling of the German battleship *Tirpitz* by *X.6* and *X.7* in September 1943.

Japan was another pioneer of the midget submarine with the excellent *Ko-Hyoteki* craft. These craft were never properly employed, however, and as Japan's military fortunes declined, the Japanese Navy began to pay more attention to craft such as the *Kaiten* and *Kairyu*. These were suicide weapons intended to overwhelm the American advance through sheer weight of numbers. Although the idea of suicide is abhorrent to those brought up in the western, Christian tradition, it was not so in Japan where the fighting forces were imbued with the idea that 'duty is more weighty than a mountain; death is no heavier than a feather'. Indeed one of the first *Kaiten* operators took as his motto the old samurai saying that he wished he had 'but seven lives to give for his Emperor'. Despite their undoubted bravery the *Kaiten*s failed to affect the war since the Americans enjoyed an overwhelming superiority in anti-submarine forces.

Germany was the last of the belligerents to employ midget submarines. Like the Royal Navy, the Kriegsmarine was unenthusiastic about midget submarines while the U-boats were scoring significant successes in the Atlantic. Faced with the prospect of an Allied invasion of Europe, the German attitude changed. The invasion fleets had to be stopped and so the ideas of a few individualistic officers about the use of midgets were taken up. In many ways the German position was similar to that of Japan. The German decision to adopt midgets was an admission that their naval strategy had failed. German midgets were weapons of desperation, founded on the hope that if used in sufficient numbers they could interupt the Allied supply line to Europe. Wih the exception of the excellent *Seehund* two-man submarine, German midget operators were hastily if not poorly trained, their craft were quickly built with little or no evaluation and most were as lethal to their crews as they were intended to be to the opposition.

In looking at midget submarine operations during the Second World War the following conclusions can be drawn. First, midget submarines have the capacity to deliver devastating blows at the enemy. Secondly, midgets are cheap and easy to build and once built are easy to conceal. Thirdly, harbour defences have never stopped a determined attack by midget submarines. The crucial factor is training and manpower. Training must be comprehensive and realistic. Likewise, a special type of individual is required for these operations and he must be possessed of exceptional qualities of determination together with professional skills of a high order. The Italian and British midget submariners succeeded largely because they were well trained. The hastily trained German and Japanese (the later Japanese weapons at any rate: the *Ko-Hyoteki* crews who attacked Pearl Harbor and Diego Suarez were dedicated professionals) did not.

The lessons of midget submarine operations during the Second World War should not be forgotten in modern times. A number of navies, particularly that of the Soviet Union, have developed midget submarines for use in war, but also for covert operations in peacetime. The threat posed by such craft is considerable, not just to prestige targets such as aircraft carriers or ballistic missile submarines in harbour, but to communication and command systems and in the insertion of special forces parties. Although the large ballistic missile and hunter-killer submarines occupy a prominent position in modern naval operations, the threat posed by their smaller brethren should not be ignored.

Special thanks are due to Gus Britton and Margaret Bidmead of the Royal Navy Submarine Museum and to Dick Boyle, engineer officer of America's only midget submarine, X.1.

4. A Russian midget submarine, known simply as No. 3, captured on the River Danube during the First World War. The Tsarist Navy possessed three such submarines which had been ordered by the Army for local defence on the Black Sea. They resembled the British 'Holland'-type submarines and were armed with two 18in bow torpedo tubes and had a crew of four. No. 3 was sent to the Danube where it was intended to use her against the highly effective Austrian Danube Flotilla. Alas, she was captured at Reni on 12 March 1918 and her subsequent fate is unclear.

5. The first success scored by a midget submarine. The Austrian battleship *Viribus Unitis* sinking in Pola Harbour on the morning of 1 November 1918. Two Italian officers, Engineer Lieutenant-Commander Raffaele Rossetti and Surgeon Lieutenant Raffaele Paolucci, used an old Mk B57 14in bronze torpedo fitted with two 170kg charges and named *Mignatta* (leech). The device was extremely simple: the two operators sat astride the torpedo or worked alongside it in the water. After penetrating the harbour defences, the two Italians succeeded in attaching one of their charges to the Austrian flagship. The warhead exploded at 0620 and the battleship rolled over and sank in little more than twenty minutes. The liner *Wien*, which was being used as a depot ship, was sunk in the same attack, being struck by *Mignatta*, still armed with her second charge and which had been wandering aimlessly round the harbour after Rossetti and Paolucci had abandoned her after being taken prisoner. The attack came too late to have any effect on the war, but it provided the inspiration for another generation of Italian human torpedomen during the Second World War.

4▲ 5▼

▲6

▲7   ▼8

6. The Japanese were the first to build midget submarines proper. Some 76 submarines of this type, *Ko-Hyoteki*, were built in great secrecy from 1934 onwards: 61 Type A, one Type B and fourteen Type C, one of which, HA-69, is shown here on its launching cradle on the deck of the transport ship *No. 5*. They were designed to be launched over the stern of their transports: a method never actually used in action. Note the two torpedoes protected by guards. The *Ko-Hyoteki* was perhaps the most advanced midget submarine in service with any navy during the Second World War. (IWM MH.6528)

7. *HA-19*, a Type A *Ko-Hyoteki*, washed ashore on the island of Oahu after the Japanese attack on Pearl Harbor in December 1941. The role envisaged for *Ko-Hyoteki* was the mopping-up of crippled American warships after the great engagement which Japan's naval leaders believed would settle the war, but in 1940 it was changed to harbour attack. Five Type A *Ko-Hyoteki* were launched against Pearl Harbor: great things were expected of them but all five were lost. Two entered the harbour and were sunk by destroyers, one was never found, the fourth sank outside the harbour and the fifth, *HA-19*, was attacked by the destroyer *Ward* and then struck a reef before drifting ashore. Her commanding officer, Ensign Kazuo Sakamaki, IJN, was captured and became the US Navy's first Japanese prisoner. (US Navy)

8. HMS *Ramillies*, the largest victim of a Japanese midget attack. On 30 May 1942 three *Ko-Hyoteki* were launched against the British anchorage at Diego Suarez, but only Lieutenant Saburo Akeida's craft made the long passage into the harbour where with one torpedo he damaged *Ramillies*, putting her out of service for nearly a year, and with his second torpedo sank the 6,993-ton tanker *British Loyalty*. Akeida and his crewman, Petty Officer Masami Takemoto, abandoned their craft and got ashore, but were shot when they refused to surrender to a Royal Marine patrol. (IWM A.23722)

9▲

9. The attack on Diego Suarez marked the high point for Japanese midget operations. As the tide of the war turned against Japan they were increasingly used in last-ditch efforts against the invasion fleets. These two Type A *Ko-Hyoteki*s lie abandoned at Kiska in the Aleutians in June 1943. The boats had been shipped to the islands to repulse an expected American invasion but were blown up and abandoned when the Japanese evacuated. Note the apertures for the two 18in bow torpedoes. (US Navy)

10. A Type C *Ko-Hyoteki* lies off Cebu in the Philippines having been abandoned in 1944 in an abortive attempt to stop the inexorable American advance. A beached Japanese transport lies behind her. Note the net cutters and jumping wire. (US Navy)

10▲   11▼

11. As the Americans drew near the Home Islands, the Japanese began mass production of midgets in a last desperate attempt to prevent invasion. This photograph shows a vast number of Type D *Ko-Hyoteki*s better known as the *Koryu* (Scaly Dragon) in a building dock at Kure at the end of the war. 540 of this type were ordered in June 1944 with a production rate of 180 per month, but only 115 are believed to have been completed: none saw action. The *Ko-Hyoteki*s were Japan's only true midget submarine: as the Americans closed in the Japanese resorted to suicide weapons. (US Navy)

▲12

12. A *Kaiten* (Heaven Shaker) goes over the stern of the cruiser *Kitakami* during trials in February 1945. *Kaiten* were one-man guided torpedoes based on the Mk 93 Long Lance torpedo and had speeds in excess of 30 knots. They could be launched over the stern of cruisers as in the photograph, but were usually carried to their objectives by submarines. In early models the operator was provided with a means of escape once he was sure his *Kaiten* would strike, although many operators would prefer to die honourably for their Emperor. Later models were purely suicide weapons. (IWM MH.6529)

13. A pall of smoke marks the spot where a *Kaiten* found a victim at Ulithi on 20 November 1944. Between 0415 and 0454 five *Kaiten* were launched by the submarines *I36* and *I47* to attack the large number of US ships in the anchorage. The *Kaiten* were easily spotted and four were dispatched by the alerted defences. One, piloted by Ensign Mishida, IJN, ran true, sinking the oiler *Mississinewa* (AO.59) with the loss of 150 of her crew. The only other victim of a *Kaiten* was the destroyer *Underhill* on 24 July 1945. The *Kaiten* was launched from a range of 1,000 yards and it is not clear whether she struck the destroyer or was herself rammed. The result was not in doubt and the 1,550kg warhead exploded, sinking *Underhill* with heavy loss of life. (US Navy)

▲13   ▼14

14. *Kaiten* mounted on the forward casing of the Japanese submarine *I370* as she sails on 20 February 1945 to attack American shipping. The *Kaiten* crews, wearing the traditional *Hachimaki* headbands and carrying their swords, are standing on their craft. Six days later on 26 February 1945 *I370* was sunk, her *Kaiten*s unused, by the destroyer *Finnegan* (DE307) 120 miles south of Iwo Jima. (US Navy)

15. A Japanese two-man *Kairyu* (Sea Dragon) abandoned in a dockyard, possibly Kure, at the end of the war. *Kairyu* were the only Japanese midget submarines designed specifically for suicide operations and were armed with either a 600kg explosive charge or two 18in torpedoes carried externally. A three-man version of the *Kairyu* was also built and fitted with a hand-raised periscope which was intended for training operational crews. No *Kairyu* were ever used in action.

16. Italy was the only other naval power which continued with the development of midgets during the inter-war period. This is an SLC (*Siluro a lenta corsa* – slow-running torpedo) but better known as a *Maiale* (pig) – preserved in the Naval Museum at Venice and typical of early Italian midgets. The prototype was completed by 1936 and like *Mignatta* carried an explosive charge at the forward end, but in this case it was a single 300kg charge. The machine also had a proper position for the two-man crew and could be steered while submerged. It was this weapon which accounted for the considerable Italian successes of the Second World War. (Museo Storico Navale, Venice)

17. The Italian submarine *Scire* showing the three pressure-tight containers on her casing for carrying three *Maiale*: two forward and one aft. *Scire* was sunk on 10 August 1942 by the British trawler *Islay*, but not before she had taken part in two *Maiale* operations. Three other boats *Ambra*, *Gondar* and *Iride*, the latter carrying four *Maiale*, were likewise converted, but *Iride* was sunk by British aircraft in the Gulf of Bomba on 22 August 1940. On 9 September 1943, *Ambra* was scuttled at La Spezia to avoid capture.

15▲

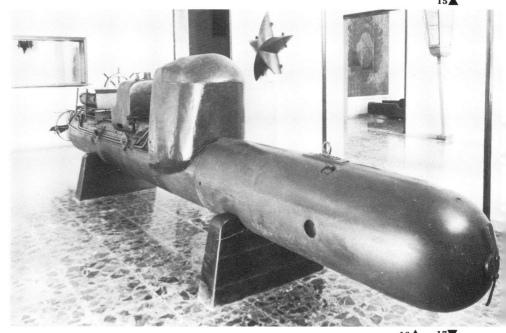

16▲   17▼

▲18

▲19 ▼20

18. *Gondar*'s first operation ended in her loss. On 30 September 1940 she was proceeding towards Alexandria to launch her *Maiale* on a raid on the harbour, when she was detected by the Australian destroyer *Stuart* which depth-charged her to the surface where she was bombed by an RAF Sunderland of 230 Squadron. The photograph shows the submarine sinking with the containers clearly visible on her deck.

19. Gibraltar harbour was the scene for the next midget attack which was also a failure. The two *Maiale* were detected and one, shown in the photograph, was later recovered by divers; the other was later washed ashore in Spain near La Linea. However, just over a year later on 20 September 1941, *Scire* delivered three *Maiale* to Gibraltar where they damaged a valuable Royal Fleet Auxiliary, the *Denbydale*, the merchant ship *Durham* and sank the storage hulk *Fiona Shell* with nearly 1,000 tons of fuel oil onboard, totalling some 28,000 tons.

20. The Italian tanker *Olterra* at Algeciras. Three further attacks were made on the anchorage at Gibraltar but none from a submarine. Instead *Olterra*, which had been interned at Algeciras since war was declared, was converted to act as a forward base with the full knowledge of the Spanish authorities. Throughout the early part of 1942 engineers laboured to convert the tanker's forepeak to a workshop and exit/re-entry compartment for the *Maiale*.

21, 22. The interior of *Olterra*'s workshop photographed in 1943 after the Royal Navy had taken over the ship, and a detailed view of the exit port in the ship's side. The first attack launched from *Olterra* on 7 December 1942 was a failure: one of the craft was captured, another returned but with only one of the two crewmen and the third disappeared. A second raid on Gibraltar on 8 May 1943 resulted in three merchant ships totalling 19,606 tons being sunk. The third attack on 4 August resulted in another three ships totalling 23,095 tons being sunk.

23. HMS *Queen Elizabeth* at anchor behind the nets at Alexandria. While the Gibraltar attacks were useful, the Italians main prize lay at the other end of the Mediterranean in the form of the British Mediterranean Fleet. The first attack in September 1940 had ended in the loss of *Gondar*. Now, in December 1941, the attempt was to be made again. The submarine *Scire* would take three *Maiale* to the island of Leros where the crews would join by flying-boat. The attack, led by Capitano di Corvetta de la Penne went in on 18 December and was a complete success. All three *Maiale* found their targets: the battleships *Queen Elizabeth* and *Valiant* were damaged as was the tanker *Sagona* and the destroyer *Jervis*. (IWM AD No. 8064)

21▲

22▲   23▼

▲24

24. Damage to the hull of HMS *Valiant* following the attack on 21 December 1941. The charge exploded under the port bulge abreast 'A' turret. The bulge was holed and forced upwards over an area of 60 feet × 30 feet. Internal damage was severe but the ship could, in an emergency, have proceeded to sea but with her fighting efficiency severely impaired. *Valiant* was back in service by July 1942. *Queen Elizabeth* was more seriously damaged with her double bottom blown in under 'A', 'B' and 'X' boiler rooms. She was out of service for 17½ months. (IWM FL.5875)

▲25   ▼26

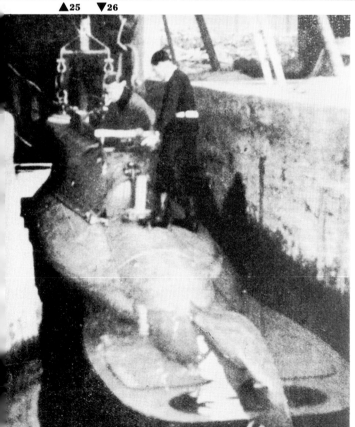

25. A modified *Maiale* at Venice in the summer of 1943. In this later variant the crew sat inside the cockpit rather than astride the machine which had a more streamlined hull form with a less pronounced fairing around the 'driver's' position than the earlier models. None was used in action. An earlier *Maiale* is shown alongside for comparison purposes. A later variant, known as SSB, was developed toward the end of the war but was never used operationally. (IWM HU.1555)

26. Italian midget development did not stop with human torpedoes. This is a very rare photograph of *CA2*, one of four *CA*-type two-man midget submarines, which was taken at the covert training base at Lake Iseo in 1942. The view is looking forward from aft and shows the hydroplanes. As built the *CA*s carried a two-man crew and an armament of two 17.7in torpedoes, but in 1941 were substantially modified. Their silhouette was drastically reduced and eight 100kg charges replaced the torpedoes, while provision was made to accommodate a third crew member – the diver, who would place the charges on the target's hull. *CA2*'s very low silhouette is very apparent in this photograph. (Dr Achille Rastelli)

27. One of the most daring Italian midget submarine operations was a plan for using a *CA*-type midget to attack shipping in New York harbour. The midget, *CA2* was the craft selected, would be taken across the Atlantic resting in a well built into the forward casing of the larger submarine *Leonardo da Vinci*. This photograph, taken at Bordeaux in September 1942, shows the well together with the two clamps which held *CA2* in position. Trials proved the arrangement to work perfectly but the plan was not implemented. (Dr Achille Rastelli)

27▲

28. The four *CA* class were followed by the *CB* design which were substantially the same although slightly larger. The photograph shows *CB10* (Costiero Tipo B–Coastal Boat Type B midget submarine), one of 22 constructed out of a projected seventy-two, Apart from being slightly larger they differed little from the earlier *CA* series (US Navy).

28▲   29▼

29. *CB* crews on a run ashore at Costanza on the Black Sea in November 1942. Six *CBs*, numbers *CB1* to *CB6*, were sent to the Black Sea to aid the Germans in the war against Russia. Their successes in this theatre were notable: *CB3* (Sorrentino) sank the Soviet submarine *S32* on 15 June 1942, *CB2* (Russo) sank the Soviet Submarine *Shch306* on 18 June 1942 and *CB4* (Sibille sank the submarine *Sc207* on 26 August 1943. (Dr Achille Rastelli)

▲30

▲31 ▼32

while *CB8*, *9*, *10*, *11* and *12* were captured at Taranto as shown in the photograph and served with the co-belligerent Italian naval forces until 1948. *CB13–CB22* were taken over by the Italian Social Republic, Mussolini's rump state in Northern Italy. All had fairly lively careers: only *CB16*, *CB19* and *CB22* survived the war. (IWM NYF.9731)

32. The Royal Navy only took to midget submarines after pressure to emulate the feats of the Italians had been applied by the Prime Minister. The British response came in two forms: first the 'Chariot', shown here being hoisted out of the water and without a warhead. (IWM HU.52449)

33. A Chariot under way on trials in Scottish waters. Note how little of the machine is visible even when running on the surface. The two-man crew both faced forward: Number One, the driver, sat in front and worked the controls with Number Two sitting behind him to help guide the craft through nets and other obstructions. (IWM A.22111)

34. The driver's position in a Chariot looking forward showing the controls. The 'helm' is centre which operated the rudder and hydroplanes with the compass positioned in front of it. The switches to left and right of the 'helm' are for controlling the ballast pumps and the handle behind the 'helm' is the main motor switch. Note also how the censor has obliterated the nature of two of the gauges in the interests of security. (IWM HU.52441)

35. A 'Charioteer' being divested of his diving-suit. A breathing apparatus modelled on the Davis Submarine Escape Apparatus was worn over the man's chest. The suit had been designed by Commander Geoffrey Sladen, a veteran submarine commander, and was known as the Sladen Suit, but soon acquired the nickname of the 'Clammy Death' suit. (IWM HU.52439)

30. *CB5* at Costanza in May 1942. Of the six sent to the Black Sea, *CB5* was torpedoed and sunk by Soviet aircraft at Yalta on 13 June 1942, but the remainder were transferred to Roumania in September 1943 on the Italian armistice and were eventually scuttled in 1944 to prevent their falling into the hands of the advancing Red Army. It is not known whether any of the craft were subsequently salvaged for examination by the Russians. (Dr Achille Rastelli)

31. Two *CB*-class submarines captured at Taranto in September 1943. The external stowage for the 21in torpedoes can be seen on both craft. Of the remaining fourteen craft, *CB7* was captured at Pola by the Germans in September and cannibalized for the spares,

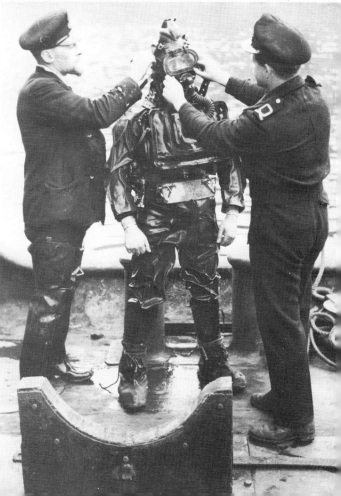

36. Like the *Maiale*, Chariots were carried to their operations by other submarines. Shown here is HMS *Trooper*, one of three T-class submarines with pressure-tight containers on their casings in which the chariots were stowed during the passage. *Trooper*, together with *Thunderbolt* and *P311*, took part in Operation 'Principal': a Chariot attack on the night of 2/3 January 1943 on Maddalena and Palermo. *P311*, the submarine ordered to launch the attack on Maddalena, was presumed mined outside the harbour. However *Thunderbolt*'s and *Trooper*'s Chariots had considerable success at Palermo. (Royal Navy Submarine Museum)

37. Lieutenant R. T. G. Greenland, RNVR, driver of Chariot XXII, who, with his Number Two, Leading Signalman A. Ferrier, successfully placed their charge under the cruiser *Ulpio Traiano* at Palermo on the night of 2/3 January 1943. They then placed explosive charges on the hulls of two destroyers and a merchant ship. The two men were able to make their way ashore where they enjoyed the satisfying sight of the explosion of their charge under Il Duce's newest cruiser. In the confusion that followed, the Italians ordered bottom searches of the other ships in harbour and the charges were discovered. (IWM A.21123)

38. Sub-Lieutenant R. G. Dove, RNVR, driver of Chariot XVI. Dove, with his Number Two, Leading Seaman J. Freel, placed their charge under the liner *Viminale* which was also badly damaged. Dove and Freel also got ashore, but all four Charioteers were subsequently captured. (IWM A.22125)

▲36 ▼37   ▼38

39. An aerial reconnaissance photograph of the harbour at Tripoli in North Africa, showing blockships sunk at the entrance to the harbour. On 18 January 1943 HMS *Thunderbolt* launched two Chariots to attack these ships and prevent their use as blockships. One Chariot had to withdraw through defects but Chariot XIII (Sub-Lieutenant H. Stevens and Chief ERA S. Buxton) pressed on but arrived off the harbour as the Germans were sinking the ships. Stevens could not attack his primary target but managed to sink the *Guilio*, his secondary target. Both men were captured and after a series of adventures sought refuge in Vatican City where they enjoyed a civilized life until the Fifth Army arrived to liberate them. (IWM CM.4694)

40. The Italian cruiser *Bolzano* sunk at La Spezia on 22 June 1944 in a joint British-Italian Chariot attack. It was feared that the Germans would sink the cruiser as a blockship so British Chariots were embarked in an Italian MTB, one designed to carry 'Pigs', for an attack on the harbour. One Chariot had to be abandoned, but the other pressed on and the charge was successfully attached to the cruiser's hull.

41. Chariots provided the inspiration for other weapons. The Motorized Submersible Canoe (MSC), better known as a 'Sleeping Beauty', was a one-man motorized canoe which could carry six limpet mines together with the operator's personal assault equipment. In this case the 'cargo' is shown strapped to the top of the canoe in front of the driver. (IWM HU.56775)

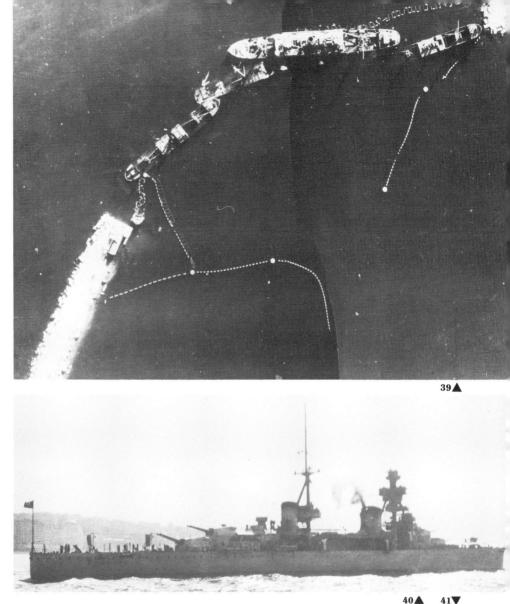

39▲

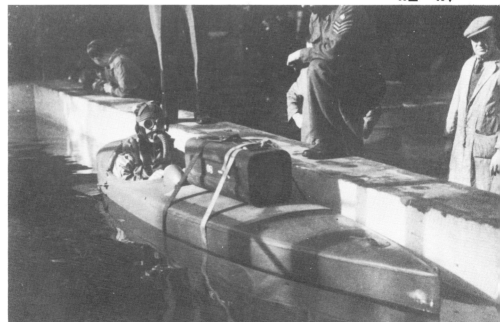

40▲   **41▼**

BRITISH CHARIOT

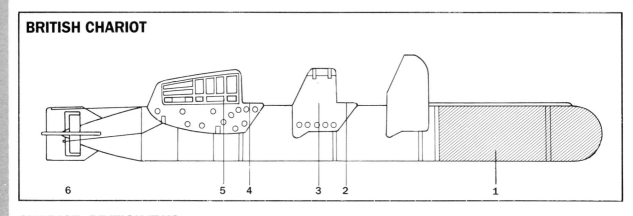

CHARIOT: BRITISH TWO-MAN HUMAN TORPEDO

1. Position where 600lb warhead would be attached.
2. Driver's ('Number One') position.
3. Ballast tank which also served as a backrest for Number One.

4. Assistant's ('Number Two') position.
5. Locker containing net cutters, magnets, ropes and two spare breathing sets which also served as a backrest for Number Two.
6. Propeller and control surfaces.
Displacement (tons): 1.5
Length (m): 7.65

Propulsion: 60 volt lead acid battery driving a 2hp electric motor
Speed (knots): 4
Range
At 4 knots: 16 nautical miles
At 2.9 knots: 17.4 nautical miles
Armament: One 600lb charge
Crew: Two

War Losses:

V	Reported in June 1944 as being in an accident off the west coast of Scotland.
VI, VIII	Lost on 31 October 1942 during Operation 'Title': an unsuccessful attack on *Tirpitz*.
X	Lost on 2 January 1943 with HM Submarine *P311* during Operation 'Principal' en route for the attack on Maddalena.
XI	Reported in June 1944 as having been abandoned at Malta.
XII, XIII	Lost on 19 January 1943 during Operation 'Welcome': the sinking of blockships in Tripoli Harbour.
XIV	Reported in June 1944 as having been abandoned at Malta.
XV	Lost on 3 January 1943 during Operation 'Principal' in the attack on Palermo.
XVI	Lost on 3 January 1943 during Operation 'Principal' in the attack on Palermo.
XVII	Reported in June 1944 as having been abandoned at Malta.
XVIII	Lost on 2 January 1943 with HM Submarine *P311* during Operation 'Principal' en route for the attack on Maddalena.
XIX	Lost on 3 January 1943 during Operation 'Principal' in the attack on Palermo.
XX	Reported in June 1944 as having been abandoned at Malta.
XXI	Reported in June 1944 as having been abandoned at Malta.
XXII	Lost on 3 January 1943 during Operation 'Principal' in the attack on Palermo.
XXIII	Lost on 3 January 1943 during Operation 'Principal' in the attack on Palermo.
XXIV	Reported in June 1944 as having been abandoned at Malta.
XXV	Reported in June 1944 as having been abandoned at Malta.
XXIX	Reported in June 1944 as having been abandoned at Malta.
XXXI	Reported in June 1944 as having been abandoned at Malta.
XXXIV	Reported in June 1944 as having been abandoned at Malta.
LII, LVII	Jettisoned on 22 November 1943 due to heavy weather during an attack on German shipping in Norwegian fiords.
LVIII, LX	Lost during the attack on La Spezia on 22 June 1944.
LXXIX, LXXX	Lost during the raid on Phuket harbour on 28 October 1944.

X-CRAFT: BRITISH THREE/FOUR-MAN MIDGET SUBMARINES

	X-Craft	XT	XE
Displacement (tons):*	26.9/ 29.7	26.7/ 29.8	30.3/ 33.6
Length (m):	15.74	15.66	16.19
Beam (m):	1.77	1.77	1.77
Propulsion:	Single shaft, one Gardner 42bhp diesel. One 30hp electric motor.		
Fuel Capacity:	2,434lb	1,134lb	2,148lb
Speed (knots)			
Surfaced:	6.6	6.6	6.6
Submerged:	5–6	5–6	5.6

Armament: Two 3,570lb charges of Amatex (Amatol plus 9 per cent RDX). Alternatively a quantity of limpet mines could be carried.

Crew: Passage crew of three: operational crew of four.

Number delivered
X-Craft: 14 boats.
XT-Craft: 6 boats with a further 12 cancelled.
XE-Craft: 11 units with one cancelled.

*Surfaced/submerged.

Schematic illustration of *X51* suspended from a crane.

1. 3,570lb explosive charge attached to hull.
2. Induction mast: in this case folded alongside the casing. In *X*, *XE* and *X51* series the induction mast could be folded as shown. In the *XT* series craft it was a fixed structure.
3. Single propeller and hydroplanes.
4. Dome for Type 151 sonar set: *X51* series only.
5. Housing for telecopic/periscopic periscope: *X51* series only. *X*, *XT* and *XE* series carried a simpler periscope only instrument.
6. Hinged antennae used for resting against target's hull while the diver attached limpet mines: *XE* and *X51* series craft only.
7. Fixed periscope used when negotiating nets or other obstacles: *X51* series only. *X* and *XE* series carried a fixed periscope further aft while the *XT* series craft did not carry such an instrument.

X3 and *X4* built by Varley Marine although *X4* was completed by the Royal Dockyard at Portsmouth and both broken up in 1945.
X5 (Vickers 1942); possibly sunk sometime around 22 September 1943 during Operation 'Source'.
X6 (Vickers 1942); scuttled on 22 September 1943 after placing her charges beneath *Tirpitz* during Operation 'Source'.
X7 (Vickers 1942); scuttled on 22 September 1943 after placing her charges beneath *Tirpitz* during Operation 'Source'.
X8 (Vickers); abandoned on 16 September 1943 during the outward passage in Operation 'Source'.
X9 (Vickers); broke her tow on 16 September 1943 during the outward passage in Operation 'Source' and was not seen again.
X10 (Vickers); scuttled on 23 September 1943 during Operation 'Source' after multiple defects prevented her reaching her operational area.
X20 (Broadbent of Huddersfield 1943); extant until October 1945.
X21 (Broadbent of Huddersfield 1943); extant until October 1945.
X22 (Markham of Chesterfield 1943); rammed and sunk by HMS/M *Syrtis* in the Pentland Firth on 7 February 1944.
X23 (Markham of Chesterfield 1943); extant until July 1945.
X24 (Marshall of Gainsborough 1943); preserved at the Royal Navy Submarine Museum.
X25 (Marshall of Gainsborough 1943); extant until October 1945.
XT1 to *XT6* all built by Vickers in 1943–4. *XT7* to *XT19* (less *XT13*) all built by Broadbent at Huddersfield but cancelled in 1944. *XT1*, *XT2* listed until October 1945, the remainder until July 1945.
XE1–*XE6* built by Vickers and all broken up in Australia in 1945.
XE7, *XE8* built by Broadbent at Huddersfield. *XE7* broken up in 1952, *XE8* preserved by Imperial War Museum.
XE9, *XE10* built by Marshall at Gainsborough. *XE9* broken up in 1952 but *XE10* cancelled while under construction. *XE11*, *XE12* built by Markham at Chesterfield. *XE11* rammed and sunk by a boom defence vessel on 6 March 1945, salved and broken up. *XE12* broken up in 1952.

X51 CLASS: BRITISH THREE/FOUR-MAN MIDGET SUBMARINES

Displacement (tons): 32/39.27
Length (m): 15.4
Beam (m): 1.8
Propulsion: One-shaft diesel electric: one Perkins P6 6-cylinder diesel plus one electric motor, 50bhp/44hp
Fuel Capacity (tons): 1.19
Speed (knots)
Surfaced: 6.5
Submerged: 6
Armament: Two detachable 2-ton side charges. Alternatively a number of limpet mines.
Crew: 5
Number delivered: Four
X51 built in 1954 by Vickers, renamed *Stickleback* in December 1954, sold in July 1958 to Sweden as *Spigger*, since 1977 preserved by Imperial War Museum.
X52 built in 1954 by Vickers, renamed *Shrimp* in December 1954, broken up at Faslane in 1966.
X53 built by Vickers in 1955, renamed *Sprat* while under construction, broken up at Faslane in 1966.
X54 built in 1955 by Vickers and renamed *Minnow* while under construction, broken up at Faslane in 1966.

BRITISH WELMAN

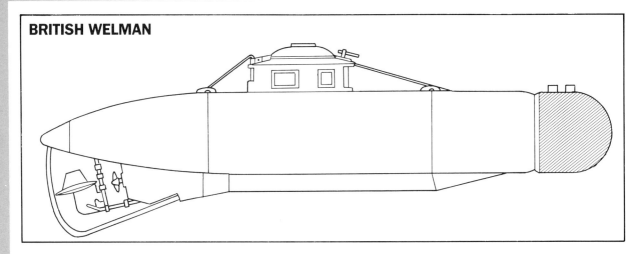

WELMAN: BRITISH ONE-MAN MIDGET SUBMARINES

Displacement (tons): 2.5 (with charge)
Length (m): 6.08
Beam (m): 1.06

Propulsion: 2.5hp electric motor
Speed (knots)
Surfaced: 3
Range (nautical miles/knots)
Surfaced: 36/4
Armament: One 540kg charge
Crew: One

Number delivered: 100+
Welman 10 lost in an accident on 9 September 1943. Welmen 45, 46, 47 and 48 all lost during the unsuccessful raid on Bergen on 21–2 November 1943. The remainder were broken up from 1944 onwards.

NEGER: GERMAN ONE-MAN HUMAN TORPEDOES

Displacement (tons): 2.7
Length (m): 7.6
Beam (m): 0.5
Propulsion: Single-shaft, one 12hp motor from electric torpedo

Speed (knots)
Surfaced: 4
Range (nautical miles/knots)
Surface: 48/4
Torpedoes: One G7e
Crew: One
Number delivered: Approx 200 plus 300 *Marders* which were identical in all

respects except that they had a displacement of 3 tons and a length of 3 metres.
Approximately 140 of the 200 *Negers* were lost in action. Of the 300 *Marders* the number lost is unclear. Roughly 150 were employed in NW Europe and the remainder in the Mediterranean.

GERMAN *NEGER*

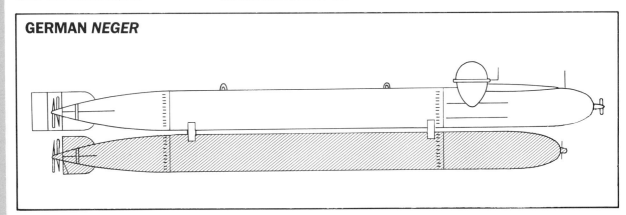

MOLCH: GERMAN ONE-MAN HUMAN TORPEDOES

Displacement (tons): 11
Length (m): 10.8
Beam (m): 1.8
Propulsion: Single-shaft, one 13hp

motor from electric torpedo
Speed (knots)
Surfaced: 4.3
Submerged: 5
Range (nautical miles/knots)
Surfaced: 50/4
Submerged: 50/5

Torpedoes: Two G7e
Crew: One
Number delivered: 383
Accurate figures for the number of *Molch* lost in action are unavailable.

GERMAN *MOLCH*

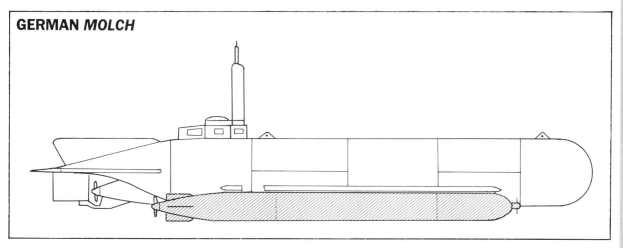

GERMAN *BIBER*

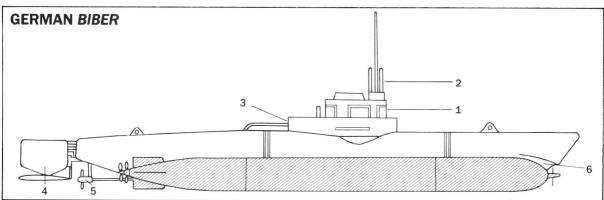

BIBER: GERMAN ONE-MAN MIDGET SUBMARINES

1. Conning tower containing glass viewing ports.
2. Masts: from forward to aft; projector binnacle; single forward-facing

3. Exhaust arrangements consisting of exhaust valve, exhaust tank and exhaust pipe.
4. Rudder and hydroplanes.
5. Single propeller.
6. Recess for G7e torpedo. The port side had a similar recess.

Photograph shows the captured *Biber 105* at Chatham in 1945 under examination by the Royal Navy. (IWM A.27770)

periscope; air induction mast.

Displacement (tons): 6.3
Length (m): 9
Beam (m): 1.6
Propulsion: Single-shaft, one 32hp Opel-Blitz Otto petrol engine. One 13hp

motor from electric torpedo
Fuel Capacity (tons): 0.11
Speed (knots)
Surfaced: 6.5
Submerged: 5.3
Range (nautical miles/knots)
Surfaced: 130/6
Submerged: 8.6/5
Torpedoes: Two G7e
Crew: 1
Number delivered: 324
Accurate figures for the number of *Biber* lost in action are unavailable.

GERMAN *SEEHUND*

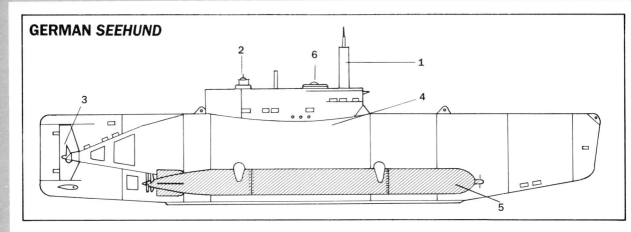

SEEHUND: GERMAN TWO-MAN MIDGET SUBMARINES

1. Housing for periscope.
2. Magnetic compass.
3. Single propeller and hydroplanes.
4. 'Saddle Tanks' to carry additional fuel.
5. G7e torpedo: equivalent on port side.
6. Conning tower hatch.

Displacement (tons): 14.9
Length (m): 11.9
Beam (m): 1.7
Propulsion: One 60bhp diesel engine with one 25hp electric motor.
Fuel Capacity (tons): 0.5
Speed (knots)
Surfaced: 7.7
Submerged: 6
Range (nautical miles/knots)
Surfaced: 300/7
Submerged: 63/3
Torpedoes: Two 53cm
Crew: Two
Number delivered: 285
Approximately 35 *Seehund* are believed to have been lost while on patrol by enemy action or as a result of bad weather and/or accident.

SEETEUFEL: GERMAN TWO-MAN AMPHIBIOUS MIDGET SUBMARINES

Displacement (tons): 20
Length (m): 13.5
Beam (m): 2.8
Propulsion: Single-shaft, one Opel-Blitz Otto petrol engine with one 30hp electric motor. Fitted with caterpillar tracks for launching and possibly bottom crawling
Speed (knots)
Surfaced: 10
Submerged: 8
Range (nautical miles/knots)
Surfaced: 300/10
Submerged: 80/8
Torpedoes: Two 53cm
Crew: Two
Number delivered: One
Tested by TVA but broken up before the end of hostilities.

MAIALE: SILURO A LENTA CORSA; ITALIAN TWO-MAN HUMAN TORPEDO

Schematic drawing of an early *Maiale* shows:
1. 220kg warhead attached to nose of the craft.
2. Driver seated astride the craft.
3. Driver's assistant.
4. Single propeller with rudder and control surfaces.
5. Ballast pump.
Length (m): 6.7
Beam (m): .53
Propulsion: One 1.6hp electric motor
Speed (knots)
Surfaced: 4.5
Range (nautical miles/knots)
Surfaced: 15/2.3; 4/4.5
Armament: Explosive charge of 220kg later increased to 250kg and finally 300kg.
Crew: 2

ITALIAN *MAIALE*

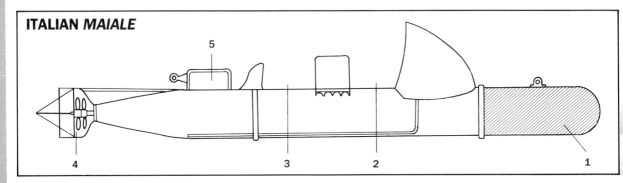

MIGNATTA: ITALIAN TWO-MAN HUMAN TORPEDO

Description: 14ft B57 (the designation B indicates that the body of the torpedo was built of bronze) torpedo with hand-holds for the two operators.
Length (m): 4.5
Range: 8–10 miles at a speed of 3–4 knots
Propulsion: Torpedo cool air engine fed by compressed air at 205 atmospheres
Warhead: Two 170kg TNT charges which were attached to the target by magnets
Crew: Two
Number delivered: Two (S1 and S2) Both constructed by the Arsenal at Venice. S1 expended on the raid on Pola, 31 October/1 November 1918. S2 preserved at the Naval Museum at La Spezia.

ALPHA, A AND B CLASS ITALIAN MIDGET SUBMARINES

	Alpha	A Class	B Class
Displacement (tons):	–	31.25/36.7	40/46
Length (m):	6.03	13.5	15.12
Beam (m):	–	2.2	2.32
Propulsion:	One electric motor	One 40/60hp electric motor	One 85bhp petrol engine; one 40–60hp electric motor
Speed (knots)			
Surfaced:	8	6.8	6.9
Submerged:	–	5.08	5
Range (nautical miles/knots)			
Surfaced:	–	12/7	128/6
Submerged:	–	8.5/4.6	9/5
Torpedoes:	–	Two 17in carried externally	Two 17.7in torpedo tubes
Crew:	1	4	5
Number delivered:	Two[1]	Six[2]	Six[3]

[1] Alpha and Beta discarded 1915–16 without being formally commissioned.
[2] A1 to A6 all built between December 1915 and March 1916 by the Arsenale at La Spezia. All were discarded on 26 September 1918.
[3] B1 to B3 built between July and November 1916 by the Arsenale at La Spezia. All three discarded on 23 January 1919. B4 to B6 were laid down at the same yard in July 1916, suspended in 1917, discarded on 23 January 1919 and scrapped from 1920 onwards.

CA (FIRST SERIES): ITALIAN TWO-MAN MIDGET SUBMARINES

Displacement (tons): 13.5/16.4
Length (m): 10
Beam (m): 1.96
Propulsion: Single shaft, one 60bhp MAN diesel; one 25hp Marelli electric motor
Speed (knots)
Surfaced: 6.25
Torpedoes: Two 17.7in torpedoes in exterior cradles. CA1 later modified to carry eight 100kg explosive charges
Crew: Two
Number delivered: Two
CA1: Built in 1938 by Caproni at Milan. Modified in 1941 and scuttled at La Spezia on 9 September 1943.

CA2: Built in 1938 by Caproni at Milan. Modified 1941–2. Was to have been used with large submarine Leonardo Da Vinci in operations off east coast of USA. Scuttled at Bordeaux in 1944, refloated in 1949 and broken up.

CA (SECOND SERIES): ITALIAN THREE-MAN MIDGET SUBMARINES

Displacement (tons): 12.8/14
Length (m): 10.47
Beam (m): 1.9
Propulsion: Single shaft, one 21KW Marelli electric motor
Speed (knots)
Surfaced: 7
Submerged: 6
Torpedoes: Eight 100kg explosive charges and twenty 2kg charges
Crew: Three
Number delivered: Two
CA3 and **CA4:** built in 1942 by Caproni at Milan. Both scuttled at La Spezia on 9 September 1943.

CB: ITALIAN FOUR-MAN MIDGET SUBMARINES

Displacement (tons): 35.96/45
Length (m): 14.99
Beam (m): 3
Propulsion: Single shaft, one 50–80bhp Diesel; one 80hp Brown-Boveri electric motor
Speed (knots)
Surfaced: 7.5
Submerged: 6.6
Torpedoes: Two 17.7in torpedoes carried in external cradles or two mines
Crew: Four
Number delivered: Twenty-two. All built by Caproni at Milan.

Number	Delivered	Fate
CB1	27 Jan 1941	Transferred to Roumania after 8 September 1943, scuttled in Black Sea in August 1944
CB2	27 Jan 1941	Transferred to Roumania after 8 September 1943, scuttled in Black Sea in August 1944
CB3	10 May 1941	Transferred to Roumania after 8 September 1943, scuttled in Black Sea in August 1944
CB4	10 May 1941	Transferred to Roumania after 8 September 1943, scuttled in Black Sea in August 1944

Number	Delivered	Fate
CB5	10 May 1941	Sunk 13 June 1942 at Yalta when torpedoed by a Soviet aircraft
CB6	10 May 1941	Transferred to Roumania after 8 September 1943, scuttled in Black Sea in August 1944
CB7	1 Aug 1943	Captured by the Germans at Pola on 12 September 1943. Transferred to the Italian Social Republic and cannibalized.
CB8	1 Aug 1943	Scrapped at Taranto 1948
CB9	1 Aug 1943	Scrapped at Taranto 1948
CB10	1 Aug 1943	Scrapped at Taranto 1948
CB11	24 Aug 1943	Scrapped at Taranto 1948
CB12	24 Aug 1943	Scrapped at Taranto 1948
CB13	1943	Captured by the Germans at Pola on 11 September 1943 while fitting out. Transferred to the Italian Social Republic and completed with parts from CB7. Sunk by Allied air attack at Pola on 23 March 1945.
CB14	1943	Captured by the Germans at Pola on 11 September 1943 while fitting out. Transferred to the Italian Social Republic and destroyed in an air raid in 1944–5.
CB15	1943	Captured by the Germans at Pola on 11 September 1943 while fitting out. Transferred to the Italian Social Republic and destroyed in an air raid in 1944–5.
CB16	1943	Captured by the Germans at Pola on 11 September 1943 while fitting out. Transferred to the Italian Social Republic. Grounded on 1 October 1944 near Senigallia, captured by the British and subsequent fate unknown.
CB17	1943	Captured by the Germans at Trieste while fitting out. Transferred to the Italian Social Republic and renumbered CB6. Sunk by Allied aircraft on 3 April 1945 off Cattolica.
CB18	1943	Captured by the Germans at Trieste on 10 September 1943 while fitting out. Transferred to the Italian Social Republic. Sunk on 31 March 1945 off Pesaro, raised 1946 and subsequently broken up at Venice.
CB19	1943	Captured by the Germans at Trieste on 10 September 1943 while fitting out and transferred to the Italian Social Republic. Broken up at Venice in 1947.
CB20	1943	Captured by the Germans at Trieste on 10 September 1943 and transferred to the Italian Social Republic. Probably captured by Yugoslav partisans at Pola at the end of April 1945.
CB21	1943	Captured in September 1943 by the Germans at Milan. Taken by train to Pola and transferred to the Italian Social Republic. Rammed and sunk by a German MFP (naval transport) on 29 April 1945 while en route for Ancona to surrender.
CB22	1943	Captured in September 1943 by the Germans at Milan. Taken by train to Pola and transferred to the Italian Social Republic. Never completed, her wreck lay on the jetty at Trieste until c.1950 when she was acquired by the Trieste War Museum.

KO-HYOTEKI TYPE A: JAPANESE TWO-MAN MIDGET SUBMARINES

Displacement (tons): 46 submerged
Length (m): 23.9
Beam (m): 1.8
Propulsion: One 600hp electric motor. One shaft but fitted with two contra-rotating propellers.
Speed (knots)
Surfaced: 23
Submerged: 19
Range (nautical miles/knots)
Surfaced: 80/2
Submerged: 55/19
Torpedoes: Two 457mm
Crew: Two
Number delivered: 20: two unnumbered prototypes then HA1 and HA2, HA3 to HA44, HA46 to HA61.
Built from 1934 onwards by Kure Dockyard and then by a special factory solely for their construction at Ourazaki near Kure. War losses: five off Pearl Harbor on or about 7 December 1941; three at Diego Suarez on 30 May 1942; four at Sydney Harbour on 31 May 1942; eight off Guadalcanal in 1942 and three in the Aleutians in 1942–3.

KO-HYOTEKI TYPES B AND C: JAPANESE THREE-MAN MIDGET SUBMARINES

Displacement (tons): 49.75 submerged
Length (m): 24.9
Beam (m): 1.8
Propulsion: One 40bhp diesel. One 600hp electric motor. One shaft but fitted with two contra-rotating propellers.
Speed (knots)
Surfaced: 6.5
Submerged: 18.5
Range (nautical miles/knots)
Surfaced: 300/6
Submerged: 120/4
Torpedoes: Two 457mm bow
Crew: Three
Number delivered:
Type B: One unit, HA45.
Type C: Fifteen units HA62 to HA76.
All built from 1942 at the midget factory at Ourazaki near Kure. War losses: four sunk off Cebu; two sunk at Zamboanga; two off Davo in the Philippines. All lost in 1944–5, the remainder being broken up after the war.

JAPANESE *KO-HYOTEKI*

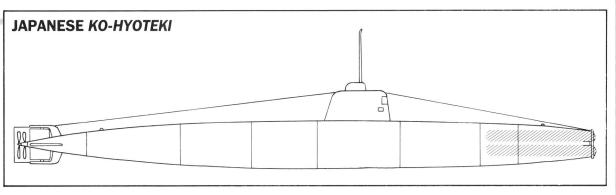

JAPANESE *KAITEN*

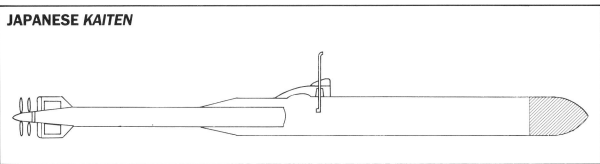

KORYU (SCALY DRAGON): JAPANESE FIVE-MAN MIDGET SUBMARINES

Displacement (tons): 58.4 submerged
Length (m): 26.25
Beam (m): 2.04
Propulsion: One 150bhp diesel. One 500hp electric motor. One shaft but two contra-rotating propellers.
Speed (knots)
Surfaced: 8
Submerged: 16
Range (nautical miles/knots)
Surfaced: 1,000/8
Submerged: 320/16
Torpedoes: Two 457mm
Crew: Five
Number delivered: 115
540 of this class were ordered with the first, *HA77*, completed in January 1945. Production problems and the effects of American bombing meant that only 115 were completed. None saw action and all were broken up in the post-war period.

KAIRYU (SEA DRAGON): JAPANESE TWO-MAN MIDGET SUBMARINES

Displacement (tons): 18.94/18.97
Length (m): 17.28
Beam (m): 1.30
Propulsion: Single shaft, one 85bhp diesel. One 80hp electric motor.
Speed (knots)
Surfaced: 7.5
Submerged: 10
Range (nautical miles/knots)
Surfaced: 450/5
Submerged: 36/3
Armament: Two 457mm torpedoes or one 600kg explosive charge.
Crew: Two
Number delivered: 212
It was planned to have 760 ready for operations by September 1945 but only 212 were ready by the end of August. All were broken up after the Japanese surrender.

KAITEN: (HEAVEN SHAKER) JAPANESE ONE-MAN HUMAN TORPEDOES

Displacement (tons): 8.2 submerged
Length (m): 14.75
Beam (m): 1
Propulsion: Single-shaft 550bhp liquid oxygen driven torpedo motor.
Speed (knots)
Surfaced: 30 knots
Range (nautical miles/knots)
Surfaced: 12.5/30
Armament: 1,550kg of explosives
Crew: One
Number delivered: c.400
Figures are for a *Kaiten* Mk 1. The Mk 2 version was similar but powered by a hydrogen-peroxide engine giving a top speed of 40 knots, but production problems prevented more than a handful being completed. *Kaiten* Mk 3 was an experimental craft which never went into production while *Kaiten* Mk 4 reverted to the liquid oxygen engine but carried a larger, 1,800kg, warhead. The total production of *Kaiten* Mks 2 and 4 is believed not to have exceeded 20. Approximately 50 of the *Kaiten*, of all types, were used operationally. Hundreds were found in Japan after the war and broken up.

WARSHIPS AND MERCHANT SHIPS SUNK BY MIDGET SUBMARINES OR HUMAN TORPEDOES

Victim	Type	Navy	Location	Date	Midget
Viribus Unitis	BB	AUT	Pola	01.11.18	*Mignatta*
Fiona shell	MV	GB	Gibraltar	20.09.41	*Maiale*
Denbydale[1]	RFA	GB	Gibraltar	20.09.41	*Maiale*
Durham	MV	GB	Gibraltar	20.09.41	*Maiale*
Sangona[1]	TKR	GB	Alexandria	19.12.41	*Maiale*
Jervis[1]	DD	GB	Alexandria	19.12.41	*Maiale*
Queen Elizabeth[1]	BB	GB	Alexandria	19.12.41	*Maiale*
Valiant[1]	BB	GB	Alexandria	19.12.41	*Maiale*
Ramillies[1]	BB	GB	Diego Suarez	30.05.42	*Ko-Hyoteki*
British Loyalty	TKR	GB	Diego Suarez	30.05.42	*Ko-Hyoteki*
S32	SM	USSR	Black Sea	15.06.42	*CB3*
SC213	SM	USSR	Black Sea	18.06.42	*CB2*
Ulpio Traiano	CR	ITA	Palermo	2/3.01.43	*Chariot XXII*
Viminale	MV	ITA	Palermo	2/3.01.43	*Chariot XVI*

A *Seehund* under inspection by Royal Navy personnel in the Konrad Bunker at Kiel in 1945.

Victim	Type	Navy	Location	Date	Midget
Camerata[1]	MV	GB	Gibraltar	08.05.43	Maiale
Mahsud[1]	MV	GB	Gibraltar	08.05.43	Maiale
Pat Harrison[1]	MV	GB	Gibraltar	08.05.43	Maiale
Thorshovdi[1]	MV	GB	Gibraltar	08.05.43	Maiale
H. G. Otis[1]	MV	GB	Gibraltar	04.08.43	Maiale
Stanridge[1]	MV	GB	Gibraltar	04.08.43	Maiale
SC207	SM	USSR	Black Sea	26.08.43	CB4
Tirpitz[1]	BB	GER	Kaafiord	22.09.43	X6/7
Barenfels	MV	GER	Bergen	13.04.44	X24
Bolzano	CR	ITA	La Spezia	21/22.06.44	Chariots LVIII/LX
Cato	MSW	GB	Normandy	06.07.44	Neger/Marder
Magic	MSW	GB	Normandy	06.07.44	Neger/Marder
Dragon[1]	CR	POL	Normandy	07.07.44	Neger
Pylades	MSW	GB	Normandy	07.07.44	Neger/Marder
Isis[2]	DD	GB	Normandy	20.07.44	Neger/Marder
Gairsay	TW	GB	Normandy	03.08.44	Neger/Marder
Samlong[1]	MV	GB	Normandy	03.08.45	Neger/Marder
Fort Lac La Ronge	MV	GB	Normandy	03.08.44	Neger/Marder
Blencathra[1]	DD	GB	Normandy	03.08.44	Neger/Marder
LCF(II) No 1	LCF	GB	Normandy	18.08.44	Neger/Marder
Quorn	DD	GB	Normandy	03.08.44	Neger/Marder
Iddesleigh	MV	GB	Normandy	17.08.44	Neger/Marder
LCF(II) No 1	LCF	GB	Normandy	18.08.44	Neger/Marder
Fration	AUX	GB	Normandy	18.08.44	Neger/Marder
Floating Dock		GER	Bergen	11.09.44	X24
Sien[2]	MV	NOR	Bergen	11.09.44	X24
Kong Oscar II[3]	MV	NOR	Bergen	11.09.44	X24
Volpi	MV	JAP	Phuket	27.10.44	Chariots
Sumatra	MV	JAP	Phuket	27.10.44	LXXIX, LXXX
Mississinewa	TKR	USA	Ulithi	20.11.44	Kaiten
Alan A Dale	MV	GB	Off Flushing	23.12.44	Biber
Heybourne Wick	AUX	GB	NNW of Ostend	02.01.45	Biber?
LST364	LST	GB	English Channel	22.02.45	Biber?
Alert	AUX	GB	English Channel	24.02.45	Biber?
Taber Park	MV	GB	North Sea	13.03.45	Seehund[4]
Newlands	MV	GB	North Sea	26.03.45	Seehund[4]
Jim	MV	GB	North Sea	30.03.45	Seehund[4]
YT17	TKR	USA	Ostend	09.04.45	Seehund[4]
Samida	MV	GB	English Channel	09.04.45	Seehund[4]
Solomon Juneau	MV	USA	English Channel	09.04.45	Seehund
Fort Wyndham	MV	GB	English Channel	11.04.45	Seehund[4]
Underhill	DD	USA	E of Okinawa	24.07.45	Kaiten
Takao	CR	JAP	Singapore	31.07.45	XE3

Key To Abbreviations:

AUT—Austria-Hungary; GB—Great Britain; GER—Germany; ITA—Italy; JAP—Japan; NOR—Norwegian; POL—Poland; USA—United States of America; USSR—Soviet Union.

BB—Battleship; CR—Cruiser; DD—Destroyer; SM—Submarine; LST—Landing Ship Tank; AUX—Naval Auxiliary; RFA—Royal Fleet Auxiliary; TKR—Tanker; TW—Trawler; MV—Merchant Vessel.

[1] Indicates the ship was damaged but not sunk
[2] Doubt exists as to whether HMS Isis was mined or succumbed to a Neger attack.
[3] Both merchant ships were destroyed in the explosion of X24's charges along with the floating dock.
[4] It is not clear as to whether a Biber or Seehund was responsible for these losses.

X1: AMERICAN EXPERIMENTAL MIDGET SUBMARINE

Displacement (tons): 31/36
Length (m): 15
Beam (m): 8.4
Propulsion: One-shaft HTP plant as completed, later replaced by a 30bhp diesel with one electric motor.
Speed (knots)
Surfaced: 15
Submerged: 12
Armament: Nil
Crew: Eight
Number delivered: One
X1 built in January 1954 by Fairchild at Farmingdale. Finally stricken on 16 February 1973.

HOLLAND-TYPE RUSSIAN MIDGET SUBMARINES

Displacement (tons): 33/44
Length (m): 20.5
Beam (m): 2.3
Propulsion: One 50bhp diesel engine. One 35hp electric motor.
Speed (knots)
Surfaced: 8
Submerged: 6
Torpedoes: Two 45cm bow torpedo tubes
Crew: Four
Number delivered: Three
All these boats built in 1913 by the Nevski Yard at St. Petersburg for the Army Ministry, to be used in local defence on the Black Sea but handed over to the Navy in 1914. No 1 was transferred to the Arctic in 1916 and lost in collision with the submarine Delfin off Murmansk on 16 April 1917. No 2 was transferred to the Arctic in 1915 and abandoned after going aground at Svjatoi on 15 October 1915. No 3 went to the Danube and was captured at Reni on 12 March 1918 by Austro-Hungarian forces. Subsequent fate unknown.

42. A 'Sleeping Beauty' under way and trimming down before diving. Propelled by an electric motor the 'Sleeping Beauty' could dive to 40 feet. 'Sleeping Beauties' were used but once, in a raid on Singapore in October 1944 led by Colonel Ivan Lyon. The party were discovered by a Japanese patrol before the attack could go in and Lyon was forced to abandon the attempt and retire after destroying the 'Sleeping Beauties'. Fourteen of the party of 24 were killed, the remainder giving themselves up to the Japanese. They were taken to Singapore where one died in captivity. The remainder were beheaded after a court-martial: their murder took place one week before the Japanese surrender. (IWM HU.56776)

▲42

43. A post-war view of a Mk 2 Chariot, known as a 'Terry' Chariot, under way in Portsmouth Harbour. As with the later variants of the Italian *Maiale*, the operators sat, back to back, inside a cockpit rather than astride the machine. 'Terry' Chariots were used only once, in the Far East in an attack on Phuket harbour on 27 October 1944. Launched from the submarine HMS *Trenchant*, the Chariots sank two merchant ships, *Volpi* and *Sumatra*. This was the only Chariot operation carried out in the Far East. The certain knowledge of what the Japanese would do to a captured Charioteer caused the cancellation of further plans for their employment.

44. The best-known and most successful Brtitish midget submarine was the X-Craft, shown here under construction at the Huddersfield yard of Thomas Broadbent in 1944. X-Craft were diesel/electric submarines carrying a crew of four: commanding officer; first lieutenant; engineer and a diver who could leave and re-enter the boat via the 'Wet and Dry' compartment to deal with obstructions or to attach limpet mines to the target's hull. Their armament consisted of two 3,570lb charges of Amatol which were carried one on each side of the submarine together with a number of limpet mines.

▲43 ▼44

45. Sub-Lieutenant Robbie Robinson standing by *X24*'s air induction mast, used when the boat was running on the surface to supply the 42bhp diesel with air and also as a voicepipe. The mast was provided with a safety rail, known as a Hezlet safety rail, after Commander Arthur Hezlet, for him to hold on to while the boat was on the surface. Forward of the induction mast is the hatch leading to the Wet and Dry compartment while aft of the mast is a non-elevating night periscope, used when on the surface at the night or for observing the activities of the diver. At the after end of the rail protecting the night periscope is the housing for the periscope proper, a 'normal' submarine's periscope in miniature and an extremely ingenious instrument. (IWM A.22905)

46. In another photograph taken for publicity purposes Sub-Lieutenant Robinson poses at *X-24*'s periscope. In front of him is the helmsman's position while behind him on each side of the boat are the release wheels for the two side cargoes: only the wheel for the starboard cargo is visible in this picture. Life in an X-Craft was cramped and uncomfortable and each had two crews; a passage crew of three – there was no diver in the passage crew – who took the boat to the operational area in the tow of another larger submarine, and the operational crew who then took the boat over for the operation itself. (IWM A.26932)

47. The German battleship *Tirpitz*, described as 'The Lone Queen of the North' but perhaps better known by Churchill's sobriquet of 'The Beast', lying behind her protective nets. In September 1943 she was lying at Kaafiord together with *Scharnhorst* and *Lützow*. It had been planned to use X-Craft against her in March 1943, but the attack was postponed due to the inadequate state of training among the crews, coupled with the approach of the long hours of summer daylight. Instead a date in September was selected and the X-Craft crews began intensive training for Operation 'Source': one of the most celebrated submarine operations of the Second World War. (IWM C.4122)

45 ▲   46 ▲   47 ▼

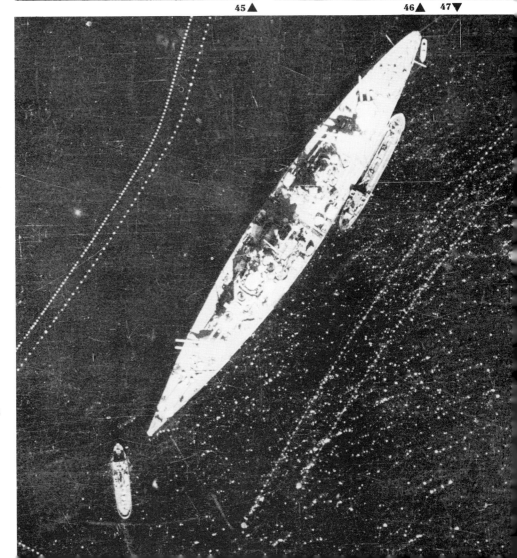

▲48

48. X-Craft commanding officers onboard the depot ship *Bonaventure* before Operation 'Source'. From left to right Lieutenant T. L. Martin, RN of *X9*, Lieutenant K. R. Hudspeth, RANVR of *X10* who were both assigned to *Scharnhorst*; Lieutenant B. M. McFarlane, RAN of *X8* whose target was *Lützow* and Lieutenant Geoffrey Place, RN of *X7* and Donald Cameron, RNR of *X6* who were both sent against 'The Beast' herself. Absent is Lieutenant H. Henty-Creer of *X5* who was assigned to *Tirpitz* with *X6* and *X7*. (IWM A.21688)

49. HMS *Thrasher* tows *X5* out of Loch Cairnbawn on 11 September to begin Operation 'Source'. The passage across the North Sea was hazardous and both *X9* and *X8* were lost. *X9* broke her tow and was never seen again, and *X8* had to be scuttled when both her charges started leaking. That left *X5*, *X6*, *X7* and *X10* to carry on the operation. Hudspeth's *X10* had to withdraw after a series of mechanical failures, but the other three successfully penetrated Kaafiord. Henty-Creer's *X5* disappeared during the operation and her fate is unclear.

▲49   ▼50   ▼51

50. Lieutenant Donald Cameron, commanding officer of *X6*, succeeded in placing both his charges under *Tirpitz* despite being hindered by a defective periscope. The Germans spotted the small craft at 0707 on 22 September and ignored her, believing her to be a porpoise. *X6* was spotted again at 0715 and this time there was no mistake, but it was too late. *X6* was too close to *Tirpitz* for her armament to bear and the hail of small-arms fire was ineffective. Cameron brought *X6* alongside *Tirpitz* abreast 'B' turret and released both charges before abandoning his small command. Cameron and his crew became prisoners-of-war, and were lucky to escape execution under the notorious 'Commando' order. Cameron was later awarded the Victoria Cross. (IWM A.21798)

51. Lieutenant Geoffrey Place, commanding officer of *X7*, who, like Cameron, was awarded the Victoria Cross, succeeded in reaching his objective. After being entangled in nets Place broke surface briefly to find himself inside the protected berth with *Tirpitz* 30 yards away. *X7* crashed into *Tirpitz* below 'B' turret where Place released one charge before going astern to release the other under 'C' turret. Onboard *Tirpitz* frantic efforts were being made to shift the ship's position but at 0812 all three charges went up causing severe damage and ending her career as a seagoing unit of the Kriegsmarine. Place was on his way out of the anchorage when his craft was severely shaken by the explosion of the charges and had to be abandoned with her crew becoming PoWs. (IWM A.21799)

52. *X24* at Port HHZ, Loch Cairnbawn, flying her 'Jolly Roger' after a successful mission to Bergen under the command of Lieutenant Max Shean, RANVR in which the 7,500-ton *Barenfels* was sunk on 13 April 1944. However Shean's target had been the nearby floating dock. The mistake was rectified on 11 September 1944 when the same submarine, now under the command of Lieutenant Percy Westmacott, returned to complete the job and at the same time have the satisfaction of observing the wreck of *Barenfels*.

53. *X23* (Lieutenant George Honour, RNR) returns to the HQ ship *Largs* on the morning of 6 June 1944 having, together with *X20* (Lieutenant K. R. Hudspeth, RANVR), spearheaded the invasion fleet by some 48 hours in order to act as navigational beacons for the landing craft heading toward *Sword* and *Juno* Beaches. For this purpose both craft were fitted with a large mast carrying a beacon, not shown here, and each flew a white ensign of a size usually only flown by capital ships, in order that there would be no mistake as to their identity.

52▲   53▼

▲54

▲55   ▼56

54. *XE6* on acceptance trials in Rothesay Bay in 1944. The eleven XE-Craft were built for service in the Far East and were slightly larger and fitted with air conditioning. They can be easily distinguished from the X- and XT-Craft by their flush casing which improved their seaworthiness. Six of the XEs went to the Pacific where they formed the 14th Submarine Flotilla and were based at Subic Bay. Their presence in the theatre was not entirely welcomed by the Americans who were lukewarm about the rather buccaneering nature of X-Craft operations. (IWM A.26930)

55. A member of the crew of an unidentified XE-Craft sitting at the hydroplane and trimming controls. The wheel on the right-hand side of the photograph is the release wheel for the starboard side cargo. (IWM A.30568)

56. The Japanese cruiser *Takao* under way in Tokyo Bay in July 1939. *Takao* was the main target for an XE-Craft raid on Singapore on 31 July 1945. *XE3* (Lieutenant I. E. Fraser, RNR) was to place her charges under *Takao* while *XE1* (Lieutenant J. E. Smart, RNVR) did the same to the cruiser *Myoko*. *XE3* successfully placed both her charges and limpet mines for good measure and got out of the harbour to rejoin her 'parent' submarine *Stygian*. *XE1* was delayed on her inward journey and since he did not know whether or not Fraser had been successful, Smart placed his charges under *Takao* before safely rejoining *Spark* for the journey back to Subic Bay (IWM MH.5935).

57. Leading Seaman Magennis (left) and Lieutenant I. E. Fraser, RNR of *XE3*. Both men were awarded the Victoria Cross for their part in the attack on *Takao* which was aptly named Operation 'Struggle'. Once inside the Singapore defences, Magennis left the craft to place his limpet mines on *Takao*'s hull, a task rendered extremely difficult because of the large amount of marine growth on the cruiser's bottom. Having placed his mines, Magennis re-entered the submarine which was now jammed under *Takao*'s bilge keel on a falling tide. Determined manoeuvring extricated the craft, but having dropped one charge, Fraser found that the second would not release, *XE3* became difficult to control and broke surface in full view of a Japanese liberty boat but, amazingly, was not detected. Fraser took *XE3* to the bottom where Magennis, despite being exhausted from his earlier efforts, left the submarine and prised the recalcitrant charge loose with a crowbar. (IWM A.26940)

57 ▲

58. HMS *Selene* preparing to take *XE5* (Lieutenant Percy Westmacott) in tow at Subic Bay in July 1945. Note the towing cable laid on *Selene*'s after casing. *XE5* was ordered to cut the Hong Kong–Singapore telegraph cable after *XE4* (Lieutenant M. Shean, RANVR) had shown that such an operation was possible by cutting the Saigon–Singapore–Hong Kong cables on 31 July. *XE5* was not as fortunate. She spent three and a half days searching for the cable with her divers working up to their shoulders in white mud. The operation was abandoned and *Selene* and *XE5* returned to Subic. After the war it was learned that *XE5*'s efforts had been successful: her nosing about in the mud and the actions of her grapple had put the cable out of action.

59. XE-Craft on the quayside at Sydney awaiting demolition after the Second World War. There was little use for the midgets in the post-war fleet where 'Austerity' was the order of the day. The six XEs employed in the Far East, *XE1*, *2*, *3*, *4*, *5* and *6*, were all broken up in Australia. In Home Waters the surviving X- and all the XT-craft were speedily paid off for disposal. *X24*, however, was preserved and is on display at the Royal Navy Submarine Museum at Gosport.

58 ▲   **59** ▼

▲60   ▼61

60. A superb view of *XE7* under way off Hampton Roads in a joint USN/Royal Navy exercise in 1950. *XE7, 8, 9* and *12* were retained in the post-war fleet and are listed as having been in commission until 1952. The aft facing hinged probe on the starboard side, when raised to the vertical, allowed the craft, with a slight positive buoyancy, to rest under the target with three feet of clearance between her casing and the target's hull, enabling the diver to exit from and re-enter the submarine to place limpet mines or deal with obstructions.

61. A diver poses at the hatch leading to his XE-Craft's Wet and Dry Compartment. The diver was an indispensable part of the crew as *XE3*'s experiences during the attack on *Takao* showed. He would exit from the craft via the Wet and Dry compartment which could be flooded up from an internal tank rather than the sea to avoid upsetting the trim. The diver knew when the compartment was full by the sudden pressure exerted on him by the incompressible water: this highly unpleasant experience was known as 'the Squeeze'. In addition to placing limpet mines on the target's hull, he could cut net obstructions away from the submarine and deal with other underwater hazards.

62. *X52*, later named *Shrimp*, one of four *X51*-class midgets built in 1954–5. Though largely similar to the XE-Craft, the four *X51*s incorporated a number of improvements. They carried an improved periscope while the induction mast could also be used as a snorkel mast with the boat at periscope depth. The night periscope was replaced by a fixed periscope right forward, used when the submarine was being guided through a net or other obstacles. The dome on the casing contains the transducer for a small sonar set, possibly a Type 151, used for gauging whether or not it was safe to come up from deep.

63. *X51*, later named *Stickleback*, under way. The four *X51*s were an unusual element in Britain's post-war submarine fleet where the operational emphasis was focused on combating the growing Soviet threat. The X-Craft force was disbanded in 1958, supposedly as a result of the Royal Navy's Submarine Service being required to delete four hulls in the interests of economy, and the deletion of the *X51*s represented the least painful way of complying. In July 1958, *Stickleback* was sold to Sweden and renamed *Spigger*. Returned to the UK in 1977, she is currently on display at the Imperial War Museum's outstation at Duxford. *X52–X54* were placed in reserve and not broken up until 1966 at Faslane.

64. The Welman one-man submarine, produced for the Army from June to August 1942 to designs by the aptly named Colonel John Dolphin. The craft were built at a hotel at Welwyn Garden City – hence their name: Welman– one–man submersible built at Welwyn. The craft were designed to be towed to their operational areas by motor boats or carried on another submarine – HMS *Thrasher* carried out the trials of this method. Welmans carried a 1,190lb charge which would be laid beneath the target and could be released from inside the craft.

62 ▲

63 ▲   64 ▼

▲65 ▼66   **67▶**

65. Lieutenant Jimmy Holmes in the small conning tower of a Welman. Welmans suffered from a number of problems which could have undoubtedly been avoided if greater thought had been given to the design. The operator sat in a very cramped position and was not provided with even the most rudimentary periscope. Instead he conned his craft by looking through the glass ports in the low conning tower with the craft partially awash. In such a condition her approach would hardly go undetected. Note also the crude 'jumping wire' stays to allow the craft to slide under obstructions and the splash guard in front of the glass observation ports.

66. A Welman on its launching cradle at Staines reservoir. The original design went through many modifications and 100 were built despite representations by the Navy on the inadequacies of the design. Welmans were used on but one operation: a raid on Bergen by four craft on 20 November 1943. They met with a singular lack of success. W46 was captured intact with her operator and the operator of another was also taken prisoner while the remaining two ditched their craft and headed for Sweden. In February 1944 the Navy advised that the Welmans be abandoned and that no attempts be made to find a more suitable use for them.

67. The Welfreighter: a two-man submersible motor boat designed for the insertion of covert reconnaissance parties. The craft is shown here being hoisted out during trials and looking from aft forward along the port side. The craft could carry cargo stowed in cylinders aft of the conning tower. The transom surrounding the cylinders could be folded down and the cargo floated ashore. Welfreighters were built at the behest of SOE for operations off Albania, but were never used in that theatre, operations there having ceased by the time they were ready. Instead a group of 6 or 8 were sent to the Far East and a small base was set up at Port Moresby in New

Guinea. It was intended to tow the Welfreighters to their operational area using 66-foot sailing ketches, but no operations were ever carried out. Despite the limited enthusiasm with which the craft was viewed during the Second World War, the underlying concept was sound.

68. Vice-Admiral Helmuth Heye, head of the German Navy's *Kleinkampfmittel-Verband* (small battle weapon force), presenting awards for gallantry. Germany was the last of the naval powers to take to midget submarines during the Second World War and there were many similarities with Japan's situation as to why the

Kriegsmarine adopted these weapons. Heye was the founder of the Kriegsmarine's midget submarine arm which he saw as a means of reversing Germany's fading fortunes at sea. Heye fostered high morale among the men who manned the various weapons devised for his command, but, as the high mortality rate among his crews was to show, failed to appreciate that no amount of morale or bravery could compensate for the lack of properly designed weapons and intensive training. (IWM HU.2246)

69. A German *Neger* (nigger), one of the first Midget weapons developed by the Kriegsmarine. It was extremely primitive and consisted of a G7e electric torpedo slung under another which had been modified to contain the one-man crew. The craft was incapable of diving but ran awash toward the target. It was very unstable especially after the lower torpedo had been released. *Neger*s were manned by volunteers from the Army and Navy, Admiral Dönitz having forbidden U-boat men to take part. *Neger*s were not suicide weapons, although their operators' assessed their chances of returning from a mission realistically: the offical odds were quoted as 50:50.

70. As shown in the photograph, the operator sat in a cockpit covered by a perspex hood which in early models could not be opened from within. He had a closed-cycle Draeger breathing apparatus, a wrist compass together with a few rudimentary controls but little else. The operator was too low down to be able to see his target properly and was often blinded by oil slicks fouling his canopy. To aim the torpedo he had a graduated scale engraved on the canopy and an aiming spike in front of him. To 'fire' the torpedo he simply released a lever and the torpedo dropped away and commenced its run. There were occasions on which the torpedo once started, failed to release from the carrier and dragged the whole craft to destruction.

68▲

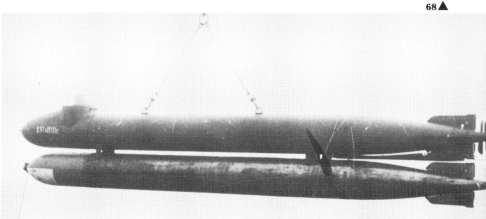

69▲   70▼

▲71

▲72　▼73

71. A *Neger* abandoned on the beach at Anzio in April 1944, the pilot having suffocated. The craft was one of seventeen *Negers* of K-Flotilla 175 which sortied from Anzio on the night of 20/21 April 1944 to attack Allied shipping. No successes were scored despite German claims. Some 200 *Neger* were built and between 60–80 per cent were lost on active service. So far as can be confirmed *Neger* successes amounted to three minesweepers and a destroyer sunk together with a cruiser and a destroyer damaged. A development of *Neger* was *Marder* (pine), similar in every respect except that it could dive to 30 metres. Some 300 *Marder* were built, but in action they were no more successful, accounting for one destroyer, one LCF and a balloon ship. (IWM NA.14029)

72. Corporal-Clerk Walter Gerhold is congratulated after returning from a *Neger* sortie off the Normandy Beaches on the night of 7/8 July 1944 in which Gerhold was credited with torpedoing the Polish cruiser *Dragon*, a feat for which he was subsequently awarded the Knight's Cross. In fact, *Dragon*'s assailant was Midshipman Karlheinz Potthast who was taken prisoner after he was found slumped exhausted in the cockpit of his *Neger* by the minesweeper HMS *Orestes* which prevented the *Neger* from getting away by riddling the craft with 20mm cannon fire.

73. The next German weapon was the *Molch* (salamander) which was an electrically driven one-man operated torpedo carrier. Ease of production was a main objective so *Molch* was designed to use as many standard torpedo parts as possible. This example was captured after the war at Kiel. Unlike the *Neger*, the operator's small conning tower was situated at the after end of the craft.

74. A *Molch* in war paint is towed ashore at TVA (Torpedoversuchsanstalt– Torpedo Test Establishment) at Eckenforde during trials in the summer of 1944. One of the two G7e torpedoes could be slung along the *Molch*'s port side. *Molch* were employed off Anzio and later off the coast of Holland; 393 were built but to little effect. The *Molch* was too complicated to operate and their crews, though undoubtedly brave, lacked proper training and support.

75. British officers examine an impressive line-up of *Molch* craft at Forus in Norway after the German surrender. The role of these *Molch* in northern waters is unclear apart from a last-ditch attempt at stopping an Allied invasion fleet. Their chances of survival in the rough northern waters would not have been high and their crews must have shed a discreet sigh of relief at news of the German capitulation. The *Molchs*' employment in that theatre indicates how the Kriegsmarine's use of midgets in the last days of the war matched that of their Japanese allies. Both nations mistakenly believed that midgets could turn the tide of war to their advantage. (IWM CL.3287)

76. The *Biber* (beaver) was a more sophisticated craft. *Biber* was a one-man craft powered by a one-shaft 32hp petrol engine – not the ideal means of propulsion for a submarine – for surface running and a 13hp electric motor for submerged drive. The armament consisted of two electric wakeless G7e torpedoes carried externally, one on each side in recesses in the pressure hull. Camouflage took many forms: in this case note the 'nest' around the top of the *Biber*'s periscope to disguise the tell-tale 'feather' when the craft was operating in rivers or close inshore. (IWM HU.56107)

74▲

75▲   76▼

77. The operator's position in a *Biber* reflecting the austere nature of the design. The control wheel is centre with the rudder indicator on lower left and hydroplane indicator at lower right. Above, from left to right, are the indicators for: engine oil pressure, oxygen pressure, battery voltage, LP air and HP air. The three armoured glass ports are visible, but the operator was also provided with a forward-facing periscope. (IWM MH.29893)

78. *Biber* were first employed off the Normandy Beaches. On the night of 29 August 1944 eighteen *Biber* of K-Flotilla 261 sailed for a raid on shipping off Le Havre. All returned and claimed a Liberty ship and a landing craft as sunk: however the exchange is not confirmed by Allied records, This was to be their only engagement for their base at Fécamp was

evacuated on 31 August and the *Biber* were abandoned on the beach as shown here. (IWM A.28252)

79. The serviceable craft were towed on trailers to a new base and, hopefully, further operations. However, their convoy was later destroyed in a night action with an American armoured column. Note that this *Biber* still has both torpedoes attached. (IWM A.28251)

80. A *Biber* washed ashore at Breskens in the Schelde Estuary. After their lack of success in Normandy, the surviving craft were sent to the Netherlands to conduct operations in the English Channel. Operations began on 23 December 1944 and *Biber*s are believed to have accounted for a net-layer, an LST and a merchant ship. The threat posed by these craft was taken seriously: offensive sweeps up the Dutch coast by MTBs had to be abandoned while they were required for hunting the *Biber*s, *Biber*s were withdrawn from operations after more than 50 had been lost and 32 men killed in two serious accidents in January and March 1945 in which torpedoes were accidently fired while the *Biber*s lay at their moorings. (IWM HU.51513)

81. The fatal consequences of the petrol engine in a *Biber*. HMS *Ready*'s motor boat approaches *Biber 90* found drifting off the North Foreland on 29 December 1944. The operator was found to have been suffocated by the fumes from the petrol engine. *Biber 90* is currently on display in the Imperial War Museum. (IWM A.28249)

▲77

▲78 ▼79

80▲   81▲

82. The Russian battleship *Arkhangelsk* (ex-HMS *Royal Sovereign*): the target for Operation 'Caesar'; a raid by six *Biber* on the Soviet anchorage at Murmansk in January 1945. The *Biber* would be carried to a position just off the Kola Inlet by three U-boats: *U295*, *U318* and *U716*; two *Biber* on each. The operation was dogged by mishaps despite intensive training by the crews. All six *Biber* were declared unserviceable en route to the objective and the operation was abandoned. (IWM A.23815)

83. A *Biber* being lowered into a Dutch canal in early 1945. *Biber*s were also employed on riverine operations, specifically in an unsuccessful attack against the bridge over the River Waal at Nijmegen on the night of 12/13 January 1945. (IWM HU.2247)

82 ▲   83 ▼

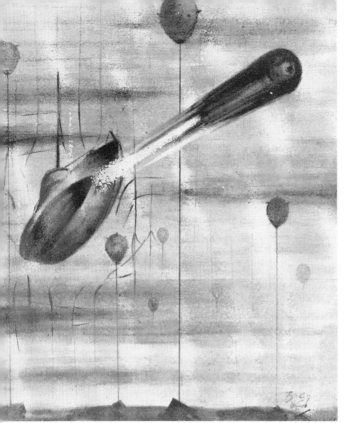

▲84

84. A German artist's impression of a *Biber* in action. As torpedo carriers they were less than successful, but they could also operate as covert minelayers, carrying an alternative armament of two mines slung one each side in place of their torpedoes. *Biber*-laid mines are believed to have accounted for nine Allied craft (seven sunk and two damaged) in operations off the Schelde. Indeed the *Biber*s might well have justified themselves if they had been restricted to the clandestine minelaying role.

85. Section of a *Seehund* captured at Kiel looking forward along the port side. The hull has been cut just forward of the diesel engine. At the top of the boat the casing has been cut away around the air intake mast, used when the boat was running on the surface. The circular structure beneath the pressure hull contains the battery troughs while on each side can be seen the recesses for the two G7e torpedoes. (IWM A.28972)

86. *Biber* was followed by the Type 127 or Type XXVIIB U-boat, better known as the *Seehund* (seal), which grew out of the Type XXVII U-boat *Hecht*. Some 53 *Hecht*s were built but used solely for training purposes. This photograph shows *Seehunden* under construction in the Konrad bunker at DWK's Kiel yard. This was the ultimate German midget submarine of the Second

▼86

▲85

World War and owed much to what the Germans had learned from sections of British X-Craft salvaged from Kaafiord. A *Seehund* carried a crew of two: commanding officer and engineer. During an attack the commander conned the boat while the engineer kept the trim and fired the torpedoes – two G7es were carried externally – on command. Unlike earlier German craft the *Seehund* had

considerable qualities of endurance and could stay on patrol for a week. (IWM A.28603)

87. Damage to the bows of HMS *Puffin* after she rammed a *Seehund* on 26 March 1945 off Lowestoft. The shock of the ramming detonated one or both of the *Seehund*'s torpedoes causing severe damage to the corvette: however, she was able

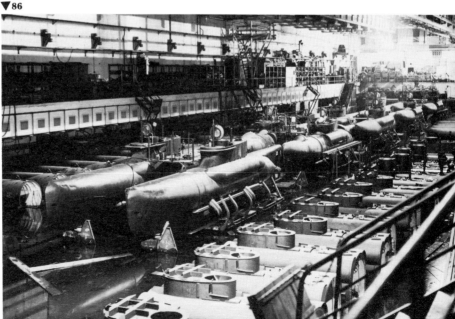

to return to Harwich under her own steam. *Puffin* later rescued three Germans from the water indicating that the *Seehund* had a passenger onboard or, more likely, that a second *Seehund* in the immediate area had sunk as a result of the torpedo explosion. Short of ramming there was little that Allied warships could do to counter the threat posed by these craft. *Seehunden* were too small to give an accurate ASDIC return and they were all but inaudible to the hydrophones of the day. (IWM A.27876)

88. The *Seehunden* came too late to influence the course of the war and most, like these two in the capable care of two Canadian provosts at Ijmuiden in Holland, fell into Allied hands at the end of the war. Twenty-three *Seehunden* were found at Ijmuiden, and a further ninety, complete with crews and equipment, were discovered at Lynaes on the north coast of Zeeland. Had these most useful submarines been available at the time of the invasion of France, they could have seriously interfered with the landings and the subsequent supply of the armies ashore. Four were taken over by the French who retained them until 1953.

89. *Seehund* was the last German midget to enter service, but by the end of the war a number of designs were on the drawing-board such as *Seeteufel* (seadevil), a two-man midget armed with two torpedoes: a model of the craft is shown here. The novel feature of *Seeteufel* was that, learning from the difficulties of getting a *Neger* or *Molch* into the water, it was fitted with caterpillar tracks to allow the craft to make its own way on land. One *Seeteufel* was built and tested by TVA at Eckenforde, but was taken to Lübeck and destroyed before the end of hostilities.

87▲

88▲ 89▼

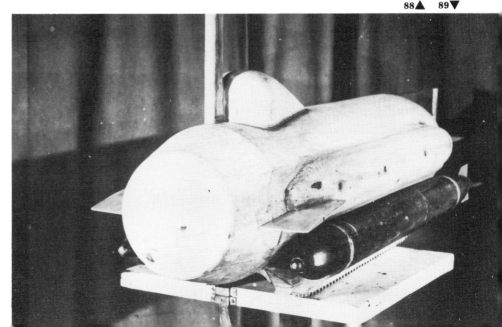

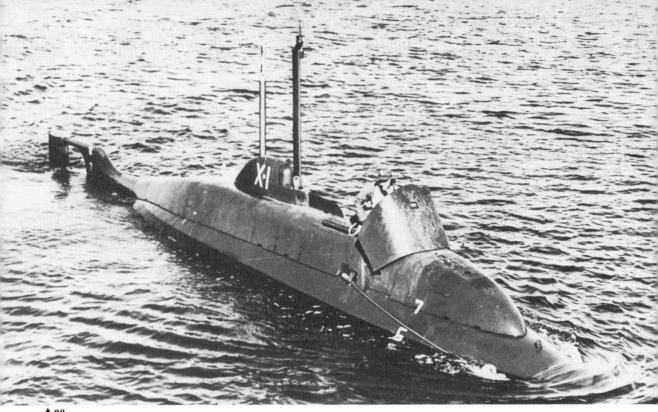

▲90

90. *X1*, America's sole
excursion into the field of
midget submarines and inspired
by the British X-Craft, one of
which had been lent to the USN
to provide design references.
She was unarmed and the
original propulsion plant used
hydrogen peroxide, a most
volatile material. After an
internal explosion in February

▼91

1958 which broke her into three
pieces, she was rebuilt but given
conventional diesel-electric
propulsion. On 14 December
1960 she rejoined the USN but
was allocated to the NSRDC as a
special test craft and painted
bright orange. As such she
survived until February 1973.
(US Navy)

91. The *Piranha*: a projected
design by the Vickers group for
a seven-man 136-ton midget
submarine capable of carrying
torpedoes or mines. Other
features of the design included
the capacity to carry a ten-man
assault group and *Piranha* was
provided with an 'exit-reentry'
compartment similar to the
'Wet and Dry' on an X-Craft for

them to leave and re-enter the
submarine. Stowage was also
provided for an inflatable craft
of Subskimmer. No orders were
recorded for *Piranha*, but
Egypt, Pakistan, Yugoslavia and
Columbia are some of the
smaller nations who
commissioned midgets in their
navies during the post-war
period.

92. A modern application of Chariot techniques. The Subskimmer: a high-speed, semi-inflatable submersible craft used for carrying frogmen from their parent submarine to their target. During the operation the craft can be 'parked' on the bottom to be retrieved afterwards. Subskimmers could be carried in pressure-tight containers on a submarine's casing, using the submarine's HP air system to inflate the craft. The photograph shows the craft being deflated during a demonstration at Portsmouth.

93. A Soviet *India*-class rescue submarine at sea. The USSR possesses two such diesel-electric submarines, one with the Northern Fleet and the other in the Pacific, which are

officially listed as being built for rescue duties, hence the carrying of two DSRVs (Deep Submergence Rescue Vehicles) on her after casing. Such a submarine could easily carry midgets in place of the DSRVs. The Soviets profited from the acquisition, by fair means or otherwise, of German and Japanese plans for midget submarines and *Jane's Fighting Ships* currently lists more than a dozen types believed to be in service or under evaluation with the Red Fleet. (US Navy)

94. The British submarine base at Faslane on the Clyde, HMS *Neptune*, where the four Polaris submarines are currently based together with other nuclear and conventional submarines and which will soon become the home for the four Trident-armed submarines currently under construction. The complex, with the associated American facility at Holy Loch, or any other SSBN base would be a prime target for any midget attack. Modern anti-submarine warfare techniques concentrate on hunting large submarines at sea and the menace posed by the midgets has largely been ignored. Long-forgotten arts such as boom defence may well have to be rediscovered. Modern naval planners would do well to remember the achievements of brave men like Rossetti, Cameron and Saburo Akeida.

92 ▲

93 ▲   94 ▼

The *Fotofax* series

A new range of pictorial studies of military subjects for the modeller, historian and enthusiast. Each title features a carefully-selected set of photographs plus a data section of facts and figures on the topic covered. With line drawings and detailed captioning, every volume represents a succinct and valuable study of the subject. New and forthcoming titles:

Warbirds
F-111 Aardvark
P-47 Thunderbolt
B-52 Stratofortress
Stuka!
Jaguar
US Strategic Air Power:
  Europe 1942–1945
Dornier Bombers
RAF in Germany

Vintage Aircraft
German Naval Air Service
Sopwith Camel
Fleet Air Arm, 1920–1939
German Bombers of WWI

Soldiers
World War One: 1914
World War One: 1915
World War One: 1916
Union Forces of the American
  Civil War
Confederate Forces of the
  American Civil War
Luftwaffe Uniforms
British Battledress 1945–1967
  (2 vols)

Warships
Japanese Battleships, 1897–
  1945
Escort Carriers of World War
  Two
German Battleships, 1897–
  1945
Soviet Navy at War, 1941–1945
US Navy in World War Two,
  1943–1944
US Navy, 1946–1980 (2 vols)
British Submarines of World
  War One

Military Vehicles
The Chieftain Tank
Soviet Mechanized Firepower
  Today
British Armoured Cars since
  1945
NATO Armoured Fighting
  Vehicles
The Road to Berlin
NATO Support Vehicles

The *Illustrated* series

The internationally successful range of photo albums devoted to current, recent and historic topics, compiled by leading authors and representing the best means of obtaining your own photo archive.

Warbirds
US Spyplanes
USAF Today
Strategic Bombers, 1945–1985
Air War over Germany
Mirage
US Naval and Marine Aircraft
  Today
USAAF in World War Two
B-17 Flying Fortress
Tornado
Junkers Bombers of World War
  Two
Argentine Air Forces in the
  Falklands Conflict
F-4 Phantom Vol II
Army Gunships in Vietnam
Soviet Air Power Today
F-105 Thunderchief
Fifty Classic Warbirds
Canberra and B-57
German Jets of World War Two

Vintage Warbirds
The Royal Flying Corps in
  World War One
German Army Air Service in
  World War One
RAF between the Wars
The Bristol Fighter
Fokker Fighters of World War
  One
Air War over Britain, 1914–
  1918
Nieuport Aircraft of World War
  One

Tanks
Israeli Tanks and Combat
  Vehicles
Operation Barbarossa
Afrika Korps
Self-Propelled Howitzers
British Army Combat Vehicles
  1945 to the Present
The Churchill Tank
US Mechanized Firepower
  Today
Hitler's Panzers
Panzer Armee Afrika
US Marine Tanks in World War
  Two

Warships
The Royal Navy in 1980s
The US Navy Today
NATO Navies of the 1980s
British Destroyers in World
  War Two
Nuclear Powered Submarines
Soviet Navy Today
British Destroyers in World
  War One
The World's Aircraft Carriers,
  1914–1945
The Russian Convoys, 1941–
  1945
The US Navy in World War
  Two
British Submarines in World
  War Two
British Cruisers in World War
  One
U-Boats of World War Two
Malta Convoys, 1940–1943

Uniforms
US Special Forces of World
  War Two
US Special Forces 1945 to the
  Present
The British Army in Northern
  Ireland
Israeli Defence Forces, 1948 to
  the Present
British Special Forces, 1945 to
  Present
US Army Uniforms Europe,
  1944–1945
The French Foreign Legion
Modern American Soldier
Israeli Elite Units
US Airborne Forces of World
  War Two
The Boer War
The Commandos World War
  Two to the Present
Victorian Colonial Wars

A catalogue listing these series and other Arms & Armour Press titles is available on request